Eat the Flowers

Poems for the youth inside us.

By Robert E. Simpson

Illustrated by Robin T. Nelson

Leaning Rock Press, LLC
Gales Ferry, CT

Copyright © 2018 Robert E. Simpson, Esq. and Robin T. Nelson

All rights reserved. No parts of this publication may be reproduced, stored in a database or retrieval system, or transmitted, in any form or by any means, without the prior permission of the author or publisher, except by a reviewer who may quote brief passages in a review.

Leaning Rock Press
PO box 44,
Gales Ferry, CT 06335
www.leaningrockpress.com

Publisher's Cataloging-In-Publication Data
 (Prepared by The Donohue Group, Inc.)

Names: Simpson, Robert E., Esq., 1949- author. | Nelson, Robin T., illustrator.
Title: Eat the flowers : poems for the youth inside us / by Robert E. Simpson, Esq. ; illustrated by Robin T. Nelson.
Description: Gales Ferry, CT : Leaning Rock Press, LLC, [2018]
Identifiers: ISBN 9781732851900 (hardcover) | ISBN 9781732851917 (softcover) | ISBN 9781732851924 (ebook)
Subjects: LCSH: Simpson, Robert E., Esq., 1949---Poetry. Life--Poetry. | Nostalgia--Poetry. | LCGFT: Poetry.
Classification: LCC PS3619.I56395 E28 2018 (print) | LCC PS3619.I56395 (ebook) | DDC 811/.6--dc23

Dedication

To the souls

with hearts standing

askew in stark fields

bending before the howling winds

of dimly lit lives.

Table of Contents

	Page
Foreword by author	1-2
Dawn	4
Glass	5-6
Nostalgia	7
Good Humor	8
Sun Ripened People	10
Home	11
Have you ever felt it?	12
At Arm's Length	13
Should I tell you?	14
God	15
Wendy	16
Daydreaming	17
Once	18
Birthday	19
Money	20
Empty	21
Picture	22
If I	24
I would like	25
Passing time	26
Skylight	28
Together	30
Question	31
Dreaming	32
Rivers	34
Dreams	35
Faces	36

Circles	38
That Old Train	40
Ants	42
I have watched	44
Empty Hearts	45
Watchmaker	46
Our Tree	48
Stay	49
My House	50
Butterflies	52
Cut Glass	54
April	55
Running	56
Bought	57
Peek-A-Boo	58
Winter	59
What	60
Me	61-62
Finding	64
Rain	65-66
Sept. 12, 1970	67
Seaweed	68
Priest	69
When?	70
Tell me	71
Waste	72
Fini	74-76

Foreword

This is my first literary effort. I began fifty-one years ago when I began to capture my feelings and life's events as poems. About thirty years ago for some unknown reason I stopped writing and put the book aside.

Originally everything was handwritten – often on scraps of paper that I stuffed into envelopes, book jacket leaf's, photo albums or other some other convenient storage hole. Every so often I would return to the browning paper and fading ink and each time I was surprised that somehow the scraps managed to survive despite the passage of time. Occasionally, I would add a new poem to the collection or revise what was already written. Each time I read the words I was unable to conceive that anyone other than me would have the slightest interest in my feelings; so, each time, back into storage the poetry went. With each return to their cubbyholes the poems managed to survive no matter how many times I dragged them around the world.

Time has become a concern as I grow older and my friends and family made their final eternal trips. With each funeral, each flower spray and each sympathy card, I increasingly came to grips with my own mortality until I decided to organize and type the handwritten scraps. Still my mind continued to tell me that my words were of no interest to anyone, maybe no longer even to me.

When I became ill and my injuries caught up with me and the surgeries multiplied, I returned to my poems. It was time to see if anyone other than me could relate to my chronicling so many feelings, events, disappointments, remembrances, loves and lost opportunities.

I asked a friend from church, who published children's books, if she would read my poems and give me her unvarnished assessment. Robin read the poems and took the much-appreciated liberty of showing the poems to a few of her friends all of whom thought the poems were worth sharing with the world. Surprised, we began working to produce this volume.

I hope you enjoy it.

Dawn

Dawn came
with colors
as I watched
waiting for you.

When you came to me
we watched the dawn come to us
visiting us with colors
adding to the spring air.

Now I watch the sun set behind me
and stand waiting
for the new rise ahead
looking for colors red as your hair
sniffing the air for your scent
I wait fixed in my frame
for your colorful return.

Glass

In winter
We sat at our table
you drew imaginary dreams
on frosted glass.

In spring
your finger tried touching
beaded rain drops
running down the glass.

In summer
we watched sailboats
cut through waves
beyond the glass.

In fall
we adored the colors
of autumn hills
far away from the glass.

In winter
your eyes reflected back
last year's dreams
from the glass.

(cont. pg 6)

In spring
when you said it's your time
you could see my anguish
captured in the glass.

In summer
you captured the wind
scattered across whitecaps
and took your last ride.

In winter
I was at our table
without imaginary dreams
drawing my finger
across the frosted glass.

Nostalgia

Snicker
other people's joke
alive and well
in plain sight but unseen.

Climbing stairs past bare bulbs
casting shadows on couples just formed
speeding by in time without real place
is it just a prayer
Our father who art in my arm
or an olden day door
hiding old memories.

Is it nostalgia
for a place never found
before he had a bad fall.

Good Humor

Ding-a-ling
the ice cream man is here
children come to buy sticks of joy
oozing down tiny arms
smeared on pants, shirts and faces.

Old man escapes from the now
never mind tomorrow
stumbles home
depositing coins in a box
opens his can
flopping down
patched faded clothes
shoes covered with dust
mind clogged
next door works.....
having kids.

Sun Ripened People

Sun ripened people
standing staring
innocence on dove faces
rising to applaud
sun ripened people.

Stopping passing a wall
scribbling something there
epitaph for friends
warnings for me.

What do you know sun ripened people
who is younger you or me
or are we both older than those we serve
where is our experience
our books and lectures
our times we will never know
a world of dreams
of what can be
of what we will never touch.

Home

I am here
I have been there
I will return
but first I must look into a green cold
along a wet world's floor
where are you?

Concealing my maker.

I am home
where they cried out for doves
from their air conditioned safety
cars and coffee shops
screaming from my girlfriend's bed
pretending what was easy
condemning seemed better
pointing fingers at me.

Lord I can't find the sins
others say they see in me
but then Lord
I can't see beyond the make-up
or the sun ripened people.

Have you ever felt it

Have you ever felt it
when you were lost without direction
when things just came to an end
in an ocean of chance?

Have you ever felt it
when your heart could not be heard
when time was clocks unwound
and alarms unrung?

Have you ever felt it
when you left yourself
wandering forever towards folly
endlessly seeking
of what you never could have?

Have you ever felt it
wandering by your door
staring at a ragged soul
picking a blade of grass
just to hide your eyes?

Have you ever felt it
when things were so unhappy
that you took refuge alone
where water ran without sound?

Will the wind cease
when I am finally left alone
seeking shelter behind great sand dunes
alarms call my dawns
as I pass and call out to you
will you look up from the grass?

At Arm's Length

When the snow comes
does it cover you
does it drop a white cloth
over life's lines etchings
now inscribed on your face?

When snow comes
does it hide the old cans and papers
or does the trash
stick closer to your breast?

Tell me your story
while I am here
for now I have the time
to listen to your woe.

I'll tell you
things I felt and missed
when I became an old can
tossed out for scrap
waiting for new snow.

Should I Tell You?

Should I tell you
about old summers
filled with life
screaming to tell me
another time another day?
There will never be
for my time passed,
scurrying home
like sailboats before a storm.

God

God knows he made the world
and the world made man
and man made misery
high tide, low tide,
today, tomorrow,
no difference
everything comes before
the universe ends our time
and steals our noise
at the wake attended by men
who engineered their sorrow.

Wendy

Birth came that afternoon
for a man born once
but dead twice
you brought your pleasure
with the laughter in your eyes
birth came again that afternoon
when I made you laugh
when you made me smile.

Daydreaming

March winds blew songs through golden hair
flowing around her face
a birthday in April
a day in May
picnics in June
concerts in July
an eve in August
a twinkle in September
leaves in October
blown away in November
months passing on clock's tickings.

Once

Maxine in Hawaii
her book of poems cradled in her arms
reading to me her very best
her heart's secrets
while I hoped
I would join her
even if it was only for one time.

Birthday

You've told me too many times,
of how I was born at three eighteen
in the west wing.

Calling to me from your boyfriends
calling me from your coma
time has flown twenty-five more times
since three eighteen
in the west wing.

Money

It's all there somewhere.
Someone totters,
someone falls,
Legs weak, minds spinning
hunger, drive-bys,
holes in the sky.
Did it affect the money?
Check your change.

Empty

I watched lights
from a shore we passed so long ago
silhouettes from eternity
captured in our fantasy
washed clean by a tide
leaving pebbles gleaming.

Picture

Shapeless wide balls
captured with my wet lens
people shuffling along
heel sounds muffled
fading until gone
captured as wet shapeless balls
taken through my wet lens.

If I

If I looked in your eyes
would I see your light
or just a twinkling?

If I touched your face
would I feel your skin
or sense your soul?

If I drank from your glass
would I taste the wet
or savor the cooling?

If I came to you
after so much time
would I touch you
or be turned away?

I Would Like

I would like to be lost,
    with no hope of being found.

I would like to sit in a dark room,
    just to hear the quiet.

I would like to be silent,
    never criticized.

I would like to never feel or touch,
    never needing to smile.

I would like never to think,
        about those who are lost and cannot
            be found,
        are blind and alone,
        speechless with so much to say,
        in stiff bodies with minds running
            in open fields,
I will never have my courage so tested.

Passing Time

Looking at each other
trying to see beneath unspeaking eyes
never mentioning what we felt
never feeling the other's pain
we sat together each alone
thinking of a waveless sea
we read our books
passing time alone
until we saw our wrinkles grow.

Skylight

I like my skylight
I look at stars
and wonder if they love
as we loved.

I like my skylight
I look at stars
and wonder if they share
the things we shared.

(cont. pg 28)

I like my skylight
I look at stars
and wonder if they sing
to each other as we have sung.

I like my skylight
I look at stars
and wonder if they remember times past
as I when I look at the stars.

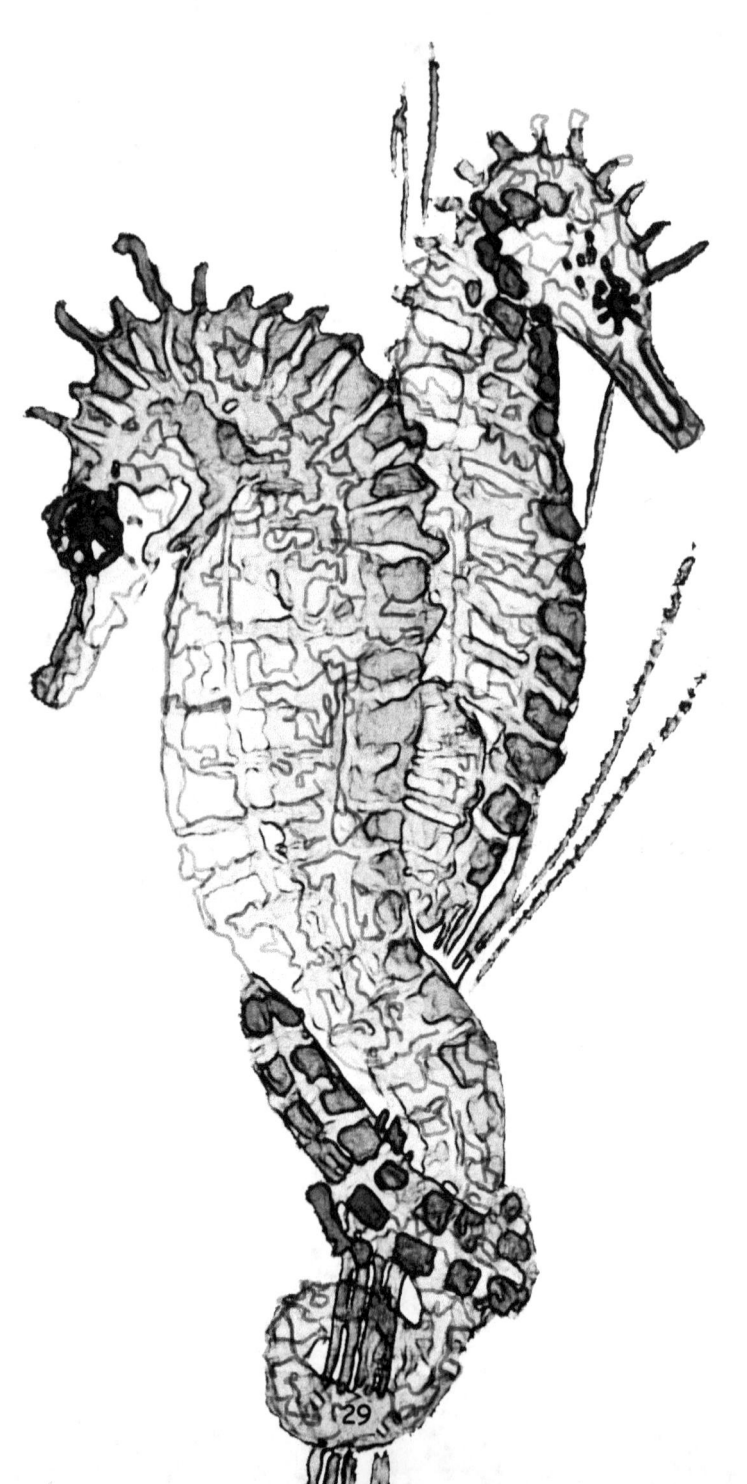

Together

We've laid together so many times
we went past counting and remembering
until we added another tick
from our minds' clocks counting down
time stopped
so we could share our spirits
before our time together
became memories.

Question

How is it someone asked
that I cannot love
don't ask
I will not answer
or allow you
to find the key to my soul.

In another time
I was afraid
it would come from the dark
sneaking up
thundering along
grabbing me
shaking me until I could feel nothing
but my fears
birthed in the same dark
that birth it.

Dreaming

Dreaming comes easy
silent dances
silhouettes on silk no real form
dreams become the center
of a life left dangling
times
wanted
hunted
never found.

Let me sleep.

Rivers

There are rivers in my mind
flowing and twisting
turning and churning
white water rapids
and deep calm pools
I ride my life out
with little stories and tricks
words and illusions
what I wanted and couldn't have
what I have and didn't want
telling of times I had and never had
wishing somehow that it would change.

Rivers never change their course
except for great hands, strong arms and work
rivers flow along
unchanging except for their banks
washed into the flow
until it reaches the sea
the silt of other lifes
settling on the bottom.

Dreams

my hours are empty
I fill time with dreams
ghostly creatures
leaping, kicking
arms flying
winds of what will never come
and never was
except in my dreams
where all is real.

Faces

I felt her eyes
fixed on me
looking into me.

I saw her face
looking back at me
so I could wonder
what her heart meant.

Am I shallow
or just hollow
to be so easily penetrated
by another.

should I call it a virtue
that I turned away
without telling her
what my heart wanted to say?

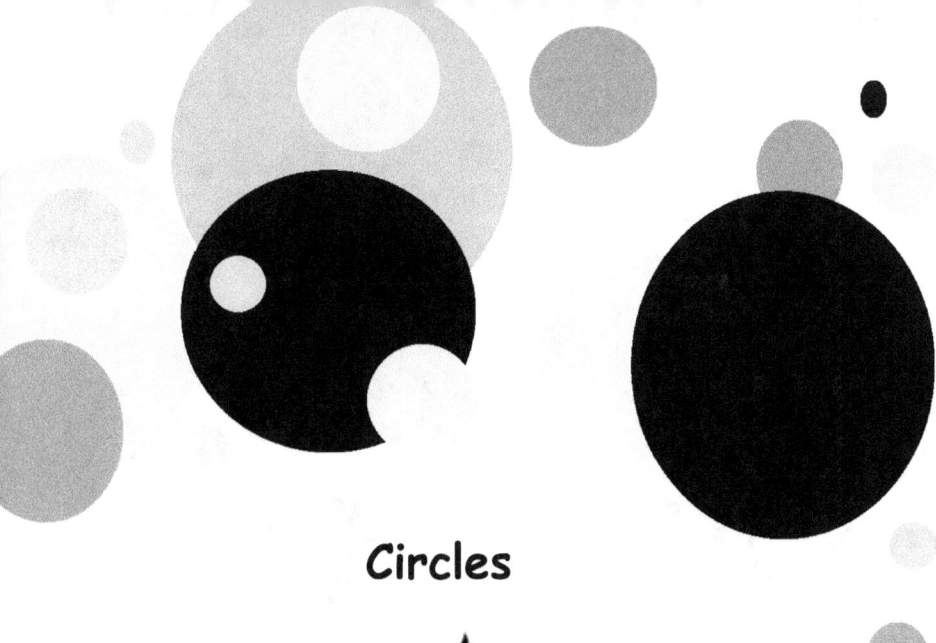

Circles

Circles keep coming
moving around and forth in my head
Circles that never begin or end
circles spinning and hurtling
through the time I have been given
to complete this life
I return to the circle
a mere spec
in endless whirling circles.

That Old Train

Wooooooooooooo
here comes that old train
steam jumping out
exploding and pushing.
Wooooooooooooooo
that old train
it rattles this old white house
shaking dishes, glasses
pushing waves across the tub.
Wooooooooooooo
that old train
big, black boiler in front
fed by sweating men
faces and bodies black with coal dust
shoveling power and life
into that old train.
Wooooooooooooo
I hear that old train
sixty years gone by
Now I feel it shake this house
like it shook that old white house
and sometimes my memories
come and go
just like that old train.
Wooooooooooooo

Ants

Like these purposeful ants
scurrying about my feet
all I do from now to tomorrow
and back to yesterday
is work for that great tomorrow
that never comes.

Creatures owning nothing more than quick jerks
half chewed leafs and a hot sting
moving and seeking
never ending searching
from hole to hole
following some ancient impulse
until that final day
when I'll just stop
and drop
into my last hole.

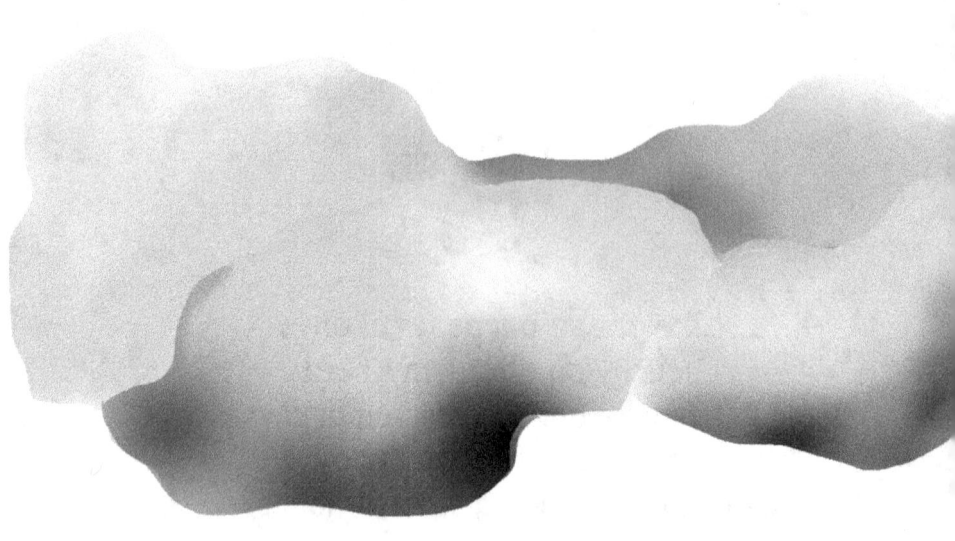

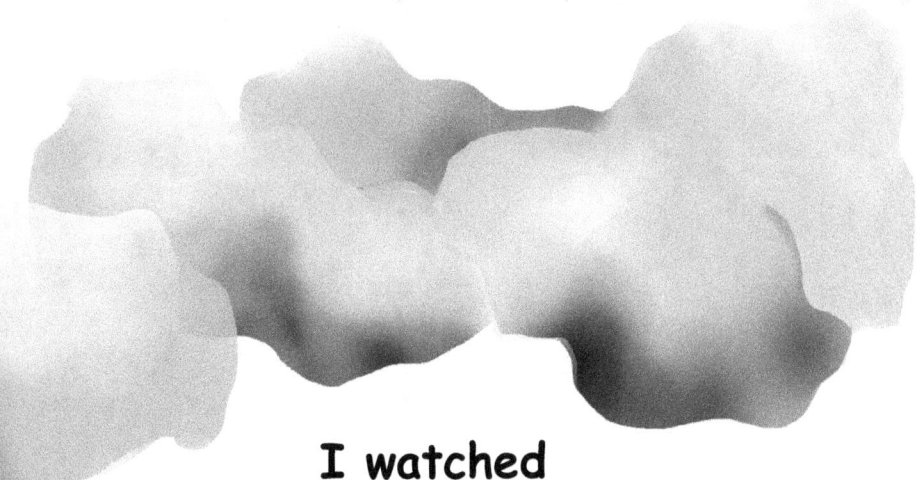

I watched

I watched the clouds pass above
pushed along by a great unseen hand
I felt how small I am
how little I mean.

I watched what seems to be
an endless parade of the white puffs
from the side of a road
where those who are never much at all
gather to watch pleasure and fame
curse others.

What is it I ask
that damns me to a world of bland days
and empty nights
while what I seek and value
curses others lives?

Empty Hearts

One of us smiled,
one of us said a kind word,
together we had a kind thought
shared a soft word
our new love gave birth to me
I looked away from you
leaving our hearts drained.

trying to save ourselves
trying to see our time
we swept ourselves away
we searched for our hidden selves
finding nothing.

Watchmaker

For the time we called ours
no watchmaker could have built
from springs and ticking things
we waited for times carefully kept
listening to thunder from inside
without dials to tell us
we soon would be gone.

Our Tree

How many times have I seen our tree
from your bedroom window
a steadfast friend
telling me I am where I belong
I wish we were a tree
too much to fade away
too big to die.

There was a thundering
before I stood outside your window
watching the light fade behind our tree
until it went out.

I wonder if I will ever again
watch our tree from your hushed room
if friendship will carry us
until we are more than our tree
or if I'll turn away
from a leafless tree.

Stay

I knew girls
    and some old women
I touched them
    told them I loved them
before I sent them away
    never asking anyone to stay
and watch with me for another day.

I asked them to stay
when the sky was dark
until new light began
when the sun grew full
we stood at the door
saying it was nice
for neither one of us
wanted the other one
beyond the dawn.

My House

My house
stood alone
a single road to its door
full of holes and ruts
littered with old bottles, boards and wires
I never bothered to clean up and cart away
I hid in my house waiting for you to come
but you would not try the road
so I sat alone
at the end of my cluttered road.

Butterflies

When fog comes
the world goes dead
when life begs for death
with a gull's cry
and butterflies quit fighting the wind
falling stiff to earth.

Cut Grass

When air smelled of fresh cut grass
I stood alone
admiring my handiwork
before I was
stuck in this life
my hand hiding my face
parting my fingers
peaking at the fresh cut grass.

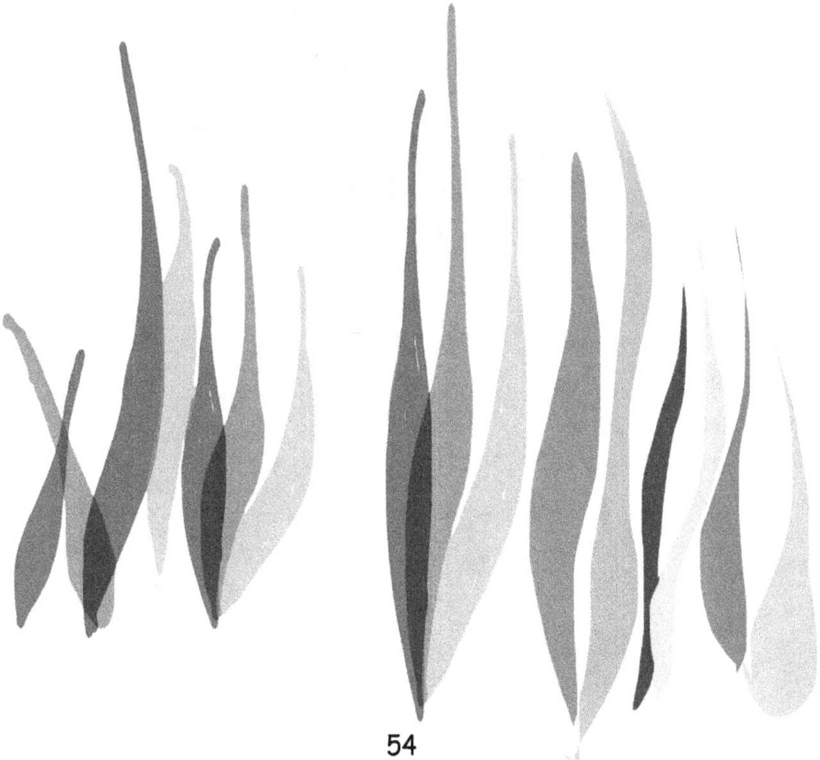

April

April has been our month
time when I first came home
alive by unseen hands
and bullets missed
time when we walked together again
along the road outside your house.

Time will be April
when we'll again walk
along a new road
with April's passed apart
left behind.

Running

It dribbled down my hair
running past my eyebrows
passing along my neck
racing down my back
across my ass
around back of my leg
out along my heel
now I know
how nice it is to feel
fresh rain running along me.

Bought

It was mine
for me to take
till I grew tired
she said I could come home for the other things
that were mine
while knowing
I was too young and proud
too afraid to say
that anything of hers
could ever be mine.

Peek-A-Boo

In the morning the sun peeks through,
playing with the shadows
dancing around my bed.

Casting off last night's mist
morning's air is filled with dawn's scent
winds of new adventures
while I lay alone and think
of the one I left behind.

I feel her warmth beside me
her strength when she took my hand
now the only rustling of the sheets
comes with the wind
and the only warmth
when the sun warms the dawn.

Winter

Winter came to us
with our frosted lips
and cold fingers
we reached out to touch
as we looked one more time
just before we said goodbye.

What

What is it that makes you you
and me me?
What is it that blows
across our faces
whispering of times past
when you were clean
and I was fresh?

Why is your sand no longer white?
That's the way I thought it was.
The way I remember it to be
in the beginning
when our souls were clean.

Me

I know a place where a battered desk sits
etched into it the scratches
of other occupants of other times
add dignity to my long ago friends.

Today while wandering and remembering my long ago
I opened a drawer revealing my long ago
forgotten
in bundled dust covered letters now brown with age
another drawer filled with pants parts
cut for some unknown reason
polish, razor blades
buttons, needles, threads,
pencils and cobwebs
jammed packed
stuffed, crammed, wrinkled
and forgotten
in my desk.

We left something everywhere we went
I wonder about me
if someone will open an old letter
stuffed in a drawer
wrinkled dusted and forgotten
and remember when I passed her way.

(cont. pg 62)

Will another light obscure my face
or a new song drown my voice
will I be just another browned photo
in an old scrapbook
someone who never meant anything
I'll be a woman's memory
of her little girl's dreams
hidden in a forgotten drawer.

Finding

Next to me
head in my arm
we watched the birds
rotate around
above our face.

You asked about my soul
something you couldn't find
something I couldn't define.

Rain

You should have seen the rain today
yes, you should have seen the rain today
it came to wash the streets
and fill gutters sloshing over curbs
spilling through metal grates
there for cabbies to splash
yes, you should have seen the rain today.

You should have watched the rain today
Yes, you should have watched the rain today
it came with thunder ripping the sky
as if God had come to call
when no man was exempt
from his symbols crashing down
Yes, you should have watched the rain today.

You should have heard the rain today
Yes, you should have heard the rain today
curious sounds made on
a symphony played on glass
beating with a drummer's precision
while window washers took vacations
Yes, you should have heard the rain today.

(cont. pg 66)

You should have felt the rain today
Yes, you should have felt the rain today
it wet my hair and lips and ran down my chin
rolling off my skin
Yes, you should have felt the rain today.

You should have seen the rain today
you have watched the rain today
you should have heard the rain today
you should have felt the rain today.

September 12, 1970

Patchwork quilt evening
sorry faces stretched across old skin
covering young faces
trying to be what we are not
unable to cover what we are.

We cannot hide
we can only hurt
even if beauty shines through
our coverup is empty
perhaps we all lie
to hide what is inside
hide our love in war
hide brotherhood in turmoil
hide our very selves
we must hide
just to be alive.

Can we be right
when we hide
society
integratescompactssocializesstandarizesdelivers
birthdayschristmaseaster
packaged humanity
bright ribbons and bows smiling
wrapped over us all.

Seaweed

I like to wander scrapping along
engulfed in a sky
surrounded by shells cast ashore
dry stringy seaweed
bleached white driftwood
polished rocks
a little treasure house
all my own
bending to pick and choose
I find peace.

Priest

A priest walked beside himself
throwing water and spiritum
in pride and dignity
proclaiming good works
ignoring corruption
working to stem the tides of now
before eternity comes around
passing without sound
striding along untarnished
holy water flying after
those fleeing the blessing
drip drying on the ground.

When?

When is our time?
Where is our place?
do we have time and place
or must we wait
while dreams turn to dust?

Do we want to dream
or be creeping feet of misty times
on rivers of swirling hurts
never expected at a beginning
but always found by the end?

Will you seek me out
to share your tenderness
or will I become
a dead tree on a barren plain?

Should we end like falling fruit
landing with a splattering noise
as its soft skin cracks
exposing tender insides
neither of us knew then
but finding too late to know?

Did we pass
without a glance when the fruit was ready
hung on branches low
awaiting our baskets?

Tell Me

Tell me all about yourself
your silly dreams and old loves
as if I really care
pour your heart out
and it will fall to the ground
another limping tale
you can pick up
dust off and shop somewhere else
maybe someone will listen
nodding his head
the illusion of concern
my attention on other parts.

Did I ever listen?
Does it matter?
Your story is painted words
colors you selected
protecting your fragile self
from another empty love
the illusion of care
dismounting when the painting is done
I caught the next bus home.

Waste

Clank
rolling around sounds
wind across pavement
trees bending
leaves blown.

Man shuffling along
worn bags and old clothes
dirty face and gritty hands
five day stubble
Mad Dog breath
behind a soft smile,

A few steps closer
a few less seconds of
time spent wandering far from a home
once had now left behind.

Fini

Winding twisting the road began
outside the gates
crossing rivers, dividing lands
people standing in twos and threes
no smiles to cover faces
just rotten teeth barred to view
nothing more than scarecrows
bleached lean skins on broken frames
continuing their dreams with vultures overhead.

Once they laughed, built and created
investigated and cried
before falling silent
to the works of their own hand.

Across the field I flew
meeting no one
their monuments still soared to the sky
pointed fingers toward a sun
awaiting their master's word
stone ears strained to hear
the laughter of a child.

(cont. pg 75)

Born of God
created by nature
begun with a thought
they all died before they could live
lunatics and brokers are all gone now
winding, twisting, their road began
finding only silence at its end.

I saw them when they plowed
smiling as they sowed
singing as they built
thinking they had life.

They came different
all wanting life to love
children to bear.

They all needed
understanding, acceptance, compassion
what each claimed to give the other
not one could ever surrender
so they asked forgiveness.

Unable to give
what each expected rendered unto themselves
they lived in worlds of noble words
and laws in books justifying it all
each remained unable to give
what they sought.

(cont. pg 76)

They stood on hind legs
thinking themselves better
while each sought eternal glory
they could not find what was inside
that could be given to all.

They stood on hind legs
thinking themselves better
while each sought eternal glory
they could not find what was inside
that could be given to all.

Unable to give
they never understood
unable to accept
they never found compassion
they walked, ran, raced
then stumbled, tottered and fell.

Now I soar above
what they plowed
what they built
what they sowed
what they missed.

SPECIAL THANKS

No one succeeds in anything without the help of others. Without the kind help of Robin Nelson, who dedicated so much of her time to illustrate and lay this book out, obtain the ISBN numbers, and guide me in this process, this book would not exist.

Leslie Woods and the people at Leaning Rock Press, LLC helped guide this effort into the form presented to you and their hard-work is truly appreciated. Other than the people who assisted in the production and printing of this book, I cannot fail to thank all of the unnamed people who have been part of my life and whose spirit is a part of the contents.

Author   Robert E. Simpson, Esq,

Bob is a Vietnam Veteran and engineer who began his military career as an enlisted man before earning a commission as a naval line officer. He became an attorney and magistrate following his active service. While in high school, his English teacher told him that he had a poet's soul and she expected him to become a poet. Thus, over fifty years ago, began the path toward this book. He began penning poems reflecting events and feelings attendant to the events that shaped his life. Bob is now disabled, married, has one daughter, three grandchildren and one great grandchild.

Illustrator   Robin T. Nelson

Robin is a children's book author and illustrator who has studied watercolor painting at the Lyme Academy of Fine Arts. She follows the color theory of the artist Stephen Quiller, with whom she has taken several workshops. She recently retired from many years as a research scientist and can now devote more time to art. Robin is a scientist at heart, a devoted wife and mother, and enjoys using her artistic skills for humanitarian purposes.

Bob Simpson   circa 1970

www.ingramcontent.com/pod-product-compliance
Lightning Source LLC
Chambersburg PA
CBHW071220070526
44584CB00019B/3093